Contents

Introduction

Welcome to the Cambridge IGCSE™ Information and Communication Technology Practical Workbook. The aim of this Workbook is to provide you with further opportunity to practise the skills you have acquired through using the IGCSE Information and Communication Technology Student's Book. It is designed to complement the third edition of the textbook and to provide additional exercises to help you in your preparation for your examinations.

The chapters in this Practical Workbook reflect the numbering and order of practical elements and chapters in the Student's Book and the syllabus – so Chapter 11 in this Workbook supports the content in Chapter 11 of the Student's Book. You will be writing your answers in this book, and as a guide there are generally two lines for each main point you need to cover – so if there are four lines you should mention two points in your answer, if there are two lines you should mention one point. However, if the answer requires only one word then there will be only one line. There is no set way to approach using this Workbook. You may wish to use it to supplement your learning of different topics as you work through each chapter of the textbook, or you may prefer to use it to reinforce your understanding as you prepare for your examinations. The Workbook is intended to be sufficiently flexible to suit whatever you feel is the best approach for your needs.

Any source files to complete questions are located at: www.hoddereducation.co.uk/cambridgeextras

11 File management

1 Explain why generic file types are used.

....

....

2 State what the following file extensions are short for:

a .rtf ....

b .csv ....

c .txt ....

d .gif ....

e .jpg ....

f .png ....

g .pdf ....

h .mp3 ....

i .mp4 ....

j .css ....

k .htm ....

l .zip ....

m .rar ....

3 Identify the **three** file types listed in Question 2 that are stored as text files and are **not** used for website authoring.

1 ....

2 ....

3 ....

4 Identify the **three** file extensions listed in Question 2 that are containers rather than files.

1 ....

2 ....

3 ....

5 Explain why version numbers should be used when saving your documents.

....

....

....

....

6 Identify **two** reasons why using smaller file sizes is desirable.

1 ....

....

....

....

2 ....

....

....

....

7 Place these files in order of the file size with the smallest first:

File A: 25MB

File B: 25GB

File C: 25KB

....

8 Explain why file compression is used.

....

....

....

....

....

....

....

....

12 Images

1 Explain the aspect ratio of an image.

....

....

2 An image is 6 cm wide by 4 cm high. It is resized to half of its original width with its aspect ratio maintained. Identify the dimensions of the new image.

a Width: ....

b Height: ....

3 Describe each of the following text wrap options when used with an image.

a In Line with Text ....

....

b Square ....

....

c Tight ....

....

d Through ....

....

e Top and Bottom ....

....

f Behind Text ....

....

g In Front of Text ....

....

4 Explain how you would place a border around an image in a document.

5 Name the type of transformation and the feature used in your word processor to turn

this image  into this one 

a Type of transformation:

b Feature used:

6 Use the file **snowman.jpg** to perform the transformation shown in Question 5.

7 Name the feature that would turn this image  into this one 

8 Use the file **snowman.jpg** to perform the transformation shown in Question 7.

9 Name the type of transformation and the feature used in your word processor to turn

this image  into this one 

a Type of transformation:

b Feature used:

10 Use the file **snowman.jpg** to perform the transformation shown in Question 9.

11 Three images – a white ellipse like that shown, but with no outside border, a photo of trees and a cartoon of a snowman are used to create the final image.

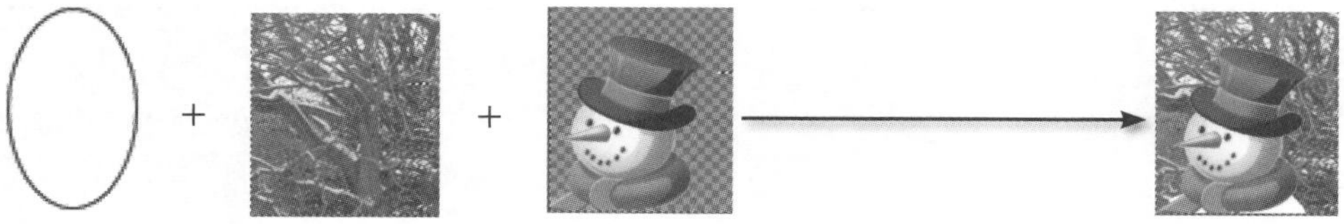

a Name the feature used to hold each image in your graphics package: ....

b Describe how this image is created.

....

....

....

....

....

....

....

....

....

....

12 Use the files **trees.jpg, snowman1.jpg** and a white ellipse to create the final image shown in Question 11.

13 Explain what resampling is.

....

....

....

....

14 Name and describe the **two** types of resampling.

1 ....

....

....

....

2 ....

....

....

....

13 Layout

1 List the **five** things you must know when planning a document.

....

....

....

....

....

....

....

....

....

....

2 What are the keyboard shortcuts for:

a Cut ....

b Copy ....

c Paste ....

d Select all ....

e Undo ....

f Redo ....

g Taking a screenshot of the whole screen ....

h Taking a screenshot of the current window ....

3 Explain what the term 'drag and drop' means.

....

....

....

....

....

....

....

....

4 Identify the type of alignment for each of these icons.

a ....

b ....

c ....

d ....

5 Identify the type of vertical alignment for each of these icons.

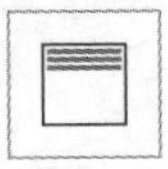

a i ....

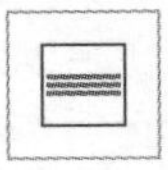

ii ....

iii ....

b State where these alignments are used.

....

....

....

....

....

....

6 Explain the following terms:

a borders ....

....

....

....

b gridlines ....

....

7 Describe how you would delete a column from the middle of a table.

....

....

....

....

....

....

....

....

8 Name the technique used to join two cells together to make a single one.

....

9 Describe how you would set the vertical alignment to the middle of a cell.

....

....

....

....

....

....

....

....

10 Define the following terms:

a header ....

....

b footer ....

....

11 Identify the **two** elements placed in the header of the pages in the Student's Book.

1 ....

....

2 ....

....

12 Identify the element placed in the footer of the pages in the Student's Book.

....

....

13 Identify **four** reasons why headers and footers are a benefit to an author.

1 ....

....

2 ....

....

3 ....

....

4 ....

....

14 Name the tab in *Microsoft Office* used to access the header and footer.

....

15 Tab stops are used to align the header and footer to a document's page margins. Identify each of the following tab stops:

a ....

b ....

c ....

d ....

16 Identify the **two** steps used to open the footer.

....

....

....

....

17 Explain why an automated date and time field might be placed in the header or footer of a document.

....

....

....

....

18 Give **three** reasons why an automated filename and file path might be included in a document header or footer.

1 ....

....

2 ....

....

3 ....

....

19 Explain why using automated page numbering is better than manual page numbering.

....

....

....

....

20 Identify the purpose of the button with the pilcrow symbol (¶) on it.

....

....

21 Identify **two** key presses in a word processor that cannot be clearly seen in a document without using the button with the pilcrow symbol (¶) on it.

1 ....

2 ....

14 Styles

1 Explain what is meant by the term 'corporate house style'.

....

....

2 List **four** elements that could be changed when applying a corporate house style to a document.

1 ....

2 ....

3 ....

4 ....

3 Apart from on documents, identify **four** places where a corporate house style may be displayed.

1 ....

2 ....

3 ....

4 ....

4 Give **four** reasons why a house style would be used.

1 ....

2 ....

3 ....

4 ....

5 Explain how a corporate house style would be applied to a company's website.

....

....

....

....

....

....

....

....

6 Describe a serif font.

....

....

7 Describe a sans-serif font.

....

....

8 Font size is measured in ....

9 The design of a typeface is called the ....

10 The height of the font is measured from the top of the ....

to the bottom of the ....

11 Describe how to use format painter when applying styles.

....

....

....

....

....

....

....

....

12 Describe bulleted and numbered lists.

....

....

....

....

....

....

....

....

13 Explain why new styles may be based on existing styles using the **Style based on:** box in the **Modify Style** window.

....

....

....

....

....

....

....

....

15 Proofing

1 Explain how a spell check program works.

....

....

....

....

....

....

....

....

2 Explain why a spell check may suggest that some words that are spelled correctly are shown as not correct.

....

....

....

....

....

....

....

....

3 Tick (✓) the correct response to complete this sentence.

Microsoft Word shows you a grammar error using

a a red wavy underline ☐

b a blue wavy underline ☐

c a green wavy underline ☐

d highlighted text ☐

4 Define validation.

....

....

5 A database on books has fieldnames and records like this.

ISBN	Author	Title	Price	Hardback	Published
978-1-471-80721-3	Brown, Watson, Sargent	IGCSE ICT	21.99	N	Y

Validation will be applied to this database. Tick if each of the following statements is true or false and for each answer state why it is true or false.

	True	False	Reason
A range check could be used to validate the title of the book			
A length check could be used to check the number of characters entered in the ISBN			
A limit check could be used for the Price field			
A consistency check could be used with the Price and Author fields			
A check digit could be added to the ISBN field			
A format check could be used with the ISBN field			
A length check could be used with the Price field			

6 List **six** proofing checks you should complete on a document, other than checking spelling, punctuation and grammar.

1 ....

2 ....

3 ....

4 ....

5 ....

6 ....

7 Identify any errors in this text:

Mr Tanton is 17 years old. She retired FROM work 6 years ago.

....

....

....

....

....

....

8 Widows and orphans can sometimes be found in word-processed documents. Explain the terms 'widow' and 'orphan'.

widow: ....

....

....

....

orphan: ....

....

....

....

9 Define verification.

....

....

....

....

10 Name and describe **two** methods of verification.

1 ....

....

....

....

....

....

....

....

2 ....

....

....

....

....

....

....

....

11 Explain, giving a suitable example, why both validation and verification do not stop all data entry errors.

....

....

....

....

....

....

....

....

12 Explain, giving a suitable example, why accidentally transposing two digits within a telephone number when entering data can cause problems.

....

....

....

....

....

....

....

....

16 Graphs and charts

1 Identify all the following graphs and charts that would be the most suitable for displaying:

a the time taken to travel different distances ....

b the percentage of people with different shoe sizes ....

c whether students travel to school by bike, car or walking ....

d a comparison of the annual sales figures for three different offices in a company ....

e the number of apples eaten this month by four students ....

f the amount spent in one year on health care by ten companies ....

g the height compared to the weight of all the students in a class ....

A B C D E F G

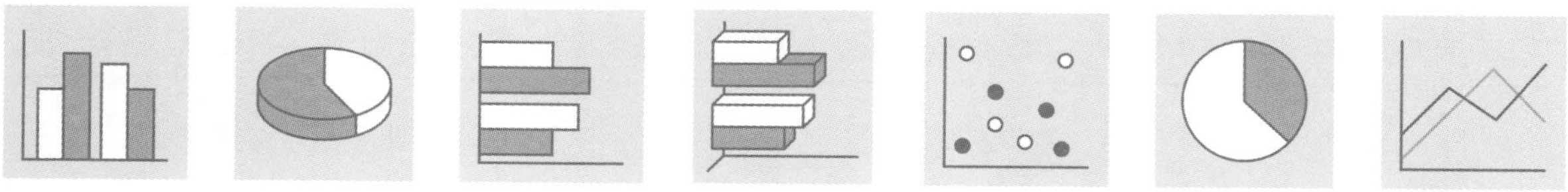

2 Which type of graph or chart would be best to compare each of the following?

a fractions of a whole ....

b the number of items sold by 20 people in one month ....

c the percentage of boys and girls in a class ....

d the temperature of water as it is heated with time ....

3 The following data will be used to create a new chart.

Distance travelled in metres	0	6	13	21	30	40	51	62	74
Time in seconds	0	10	20	30	40	50	60	70	80

a State the type of chart that will be most appropriate.

....

b Explain why this is the most appropriate type.

....

....

....

....

c Explain how this chart would be structured.

....

....

....

....

4 Identify all data in row 2 of this spreadsheet that is:

	A	B	C
1	Sales	January	February
2	Cakes	42.23	40.34
3	Fruit	52.12	12.3
4	Sweets	16	48.5

a contiguous ....

....

....

....

b non-contiguous ....

....

....

....

5 Identify the key held down to select non-contiguous data using the mouse.

....

6 Identify the items labelled on the chart below:

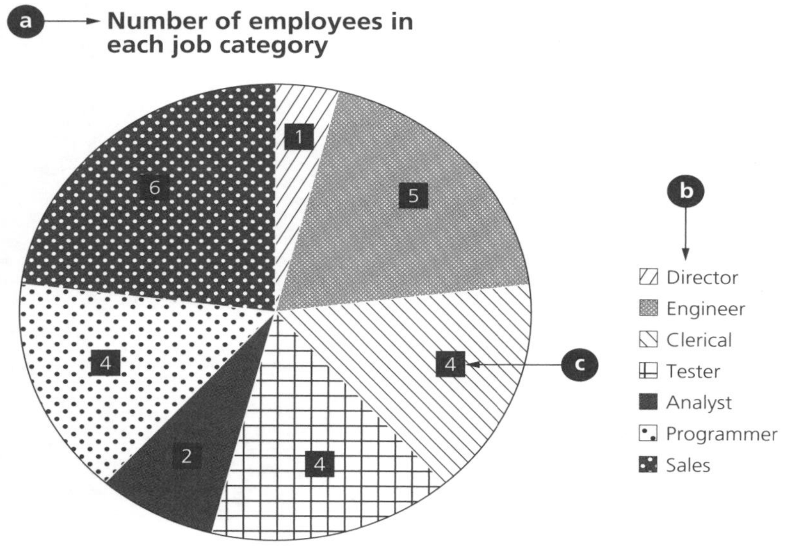

a ....

b ....

c ....

7 Identify the items labelled on the chart below:

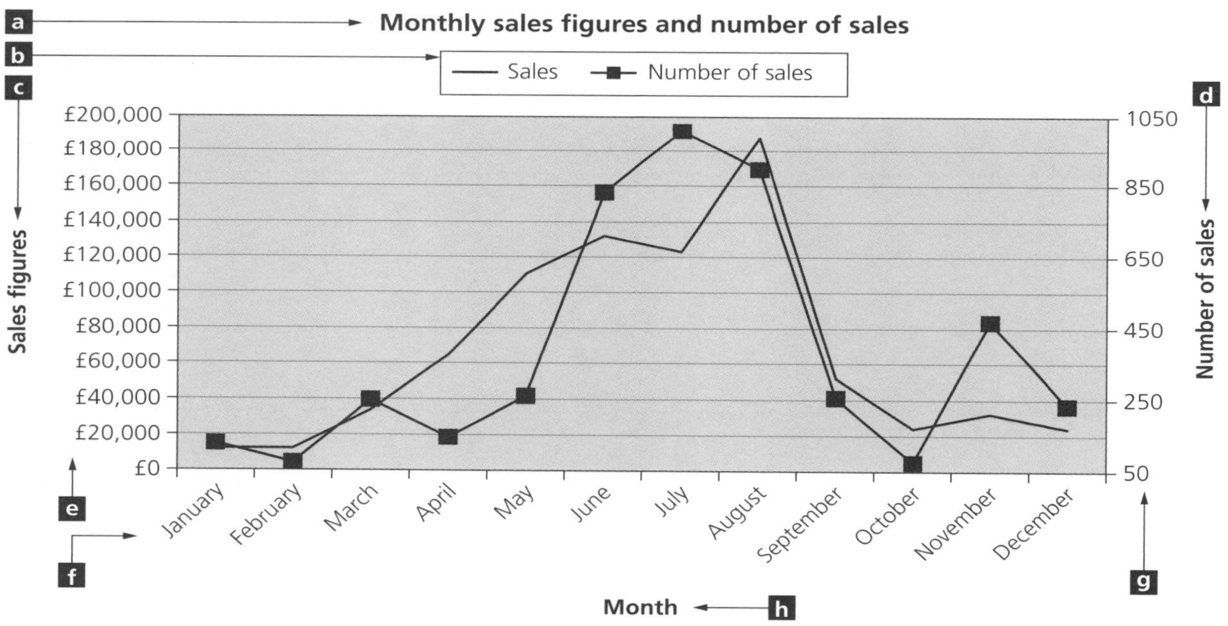

(The first one is done for you.)

a Chart title

b ....

c ....

d ....

e ....

f ....

g ....

h ....

8 Explain why secondary axes would be needed for some graphs and charts.

....

....

....

....

....

....

....

....

9 Explain what values may be changed in the secondary axis of a comparative line graph to improve its readability.

....

....

....

....

....

....

10 Describe the steps required to change the first chart to the second chart.

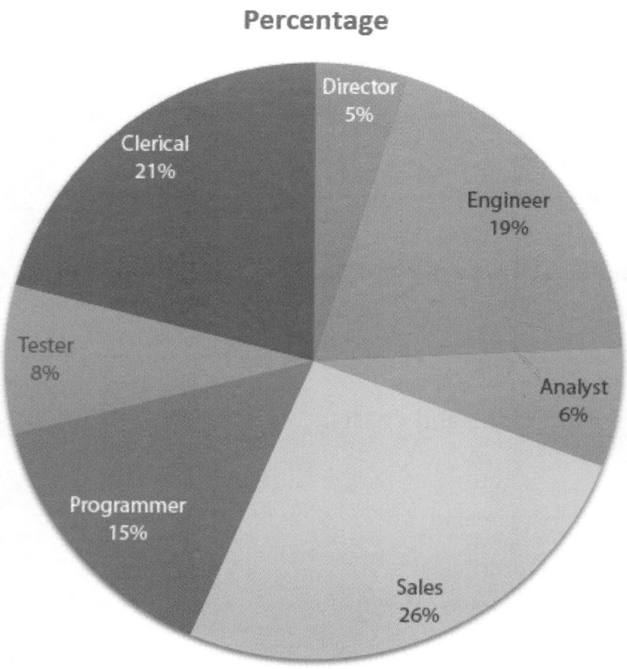

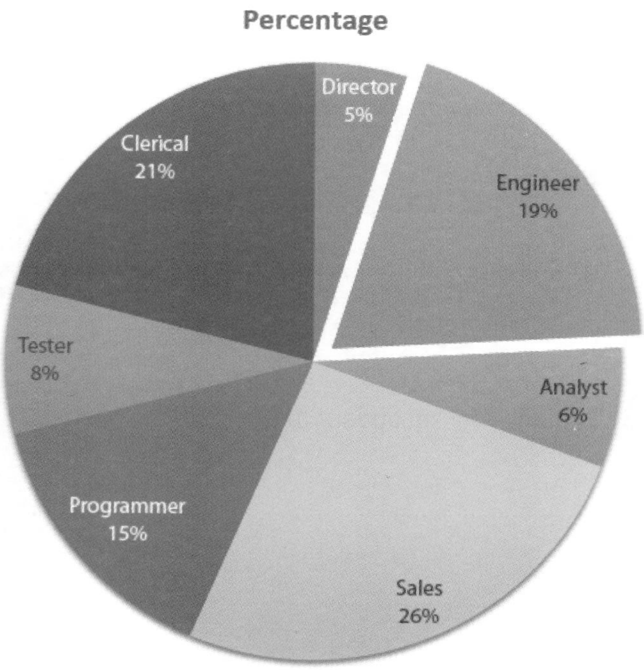

....

....

....

....

....

....

17 Document production

1 Explain the difference between files with .txt, .rtf and .docx file extensions.

....

....

....

....

....

....

2 Explain to a student how to change the paper size from A4 to A5 in your word-processing package.

....

....

....

....

....

....

....

....

3 Name the **three** tabs in the Page Setup window in *Microsoft Word*.

1 ....

2 ....

3 ....

4 Explain the meaning of the term 'gutter' within a document.

....

....

....

....

5 Describe the similarities and differences between a widow and an orphan in document production.

....

....

....

....

....

....

....

....

6 Explain the following terms:

a page break ....

....

....

....

b section break ....

....

....

....

c column break ....

....

....

....

7 Turn to page 348 of your Student's Book. Look at the image of a document in the bottom right corner.

a Fill in the missing word in the following sentence:

The yellow highlighted text is called ....

b Explain how you would improve the layout of this text without changing the styles.

....

....

....

....

8 Explain where you would find these icons in your word processor.

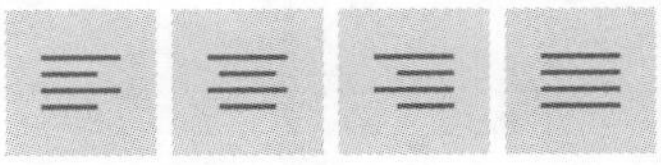

....

....

....

....

9 Explain the effect each icon has when applied to a paragraph of text:

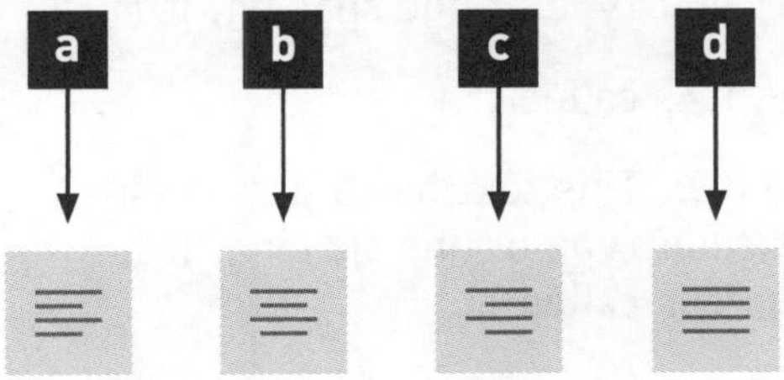

a ....

....

....

....

b ....

....

....

....

c ....

....

....

....

d ....

....

....

....

10 Turn to page 348 of your Student's Book. Look at the image of a document in the bottom right corner. Name the type of line spacing used in this document.

....

11 What type of line spacing has been used with this text:

a This text has a particular type of line spacing, it is called ... This text has a particular type of line spacing, it is called ... This text has a particular type of line spacing, it is called ... This text has a particular type of line spacing, it is called ...

b This text has a particular type of line spacing, it is called ... This text has a particular type of line spacing, it is called ... This text has a particular type of line spacing, it is called ... This text has a particular type of line spacing, it is called ...

c This text has a particular type of line spacing, it is called ... This text has a particular type of line spacing, it is called ... This text has a particular type of line spacing, it is called ... This text has a particular type of line spacing, it is called ...

d This text has a particular type of line spacing, it is called ... This text has a particular type of line spacing, it is called ... This text has a particular type of line spacing, it is called ... This text has a particular type of line spacing, it is called ...

a ....

b ....

c ....

d ....

12 Complete the following sentence:

Tabulation stops are set by placing them on the ....

13 Explain the purpose of each icon:

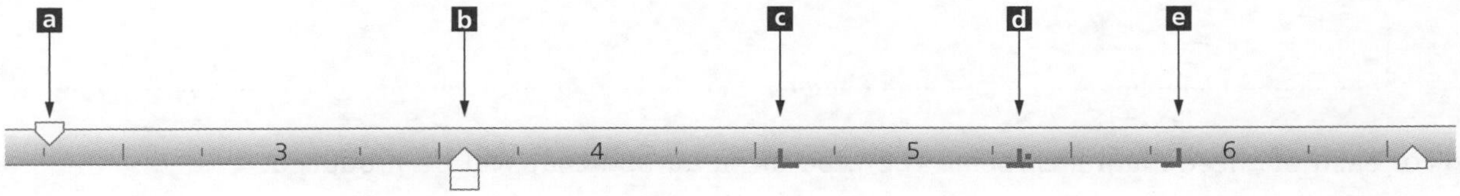

a ....

....

....

....

b ....

....

....

....

c ....

....

....

....

d ....

....

....

....

e ....

....

....

....

14 For each of these diagrams, name the type of paragraph that will be produced.

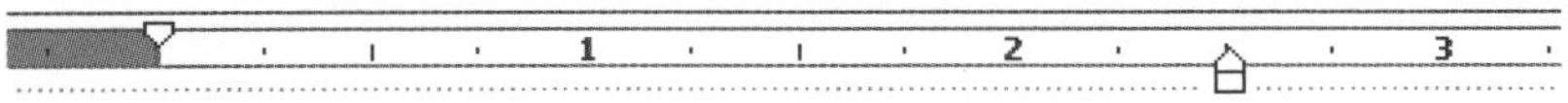

a ....

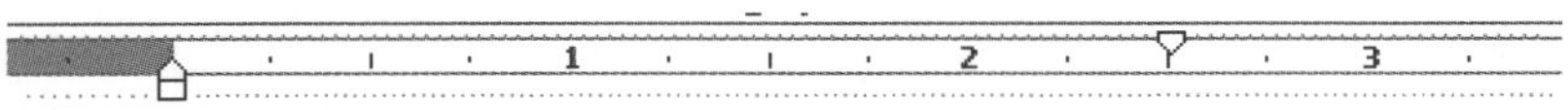

b ....

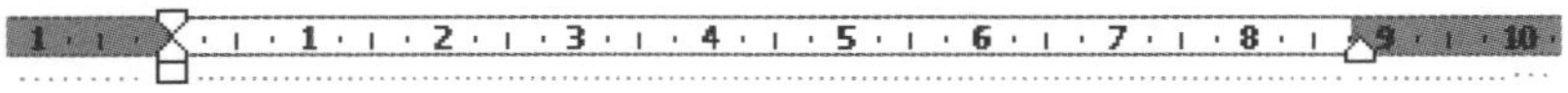

c ....

18 Databases

1 Explain the following terms:

database ....

....

....

....

database program ....

....

....

....

2 Complete the following sentences with the correct terms from the list below:

- field
- field name
- flat-file
- record
- relational
- table

a A .... database stores its data in one ...., which are organised by rows and columns.

b A .... database stores the data in more than one linked table, stored in the file.

c A .... contains data about one person or item.

d Each column in a database table contains a .... which has been given a ....

3 Label the parts of this database.

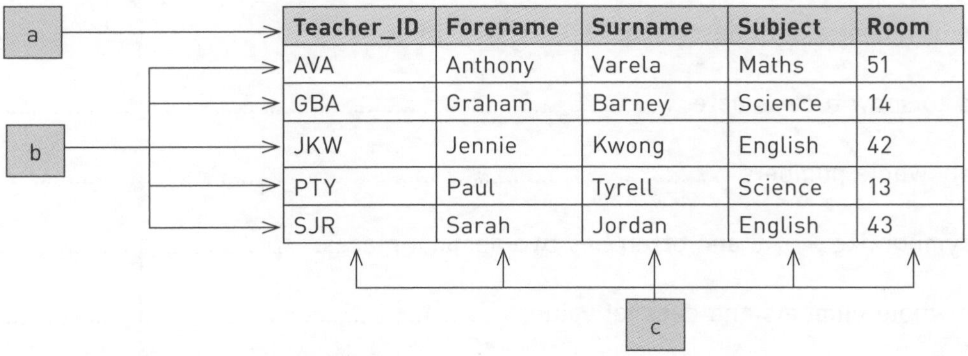

Teacher_ID	Forename	Surname	Subject	Room
AVA	Anthony	Varela	Maths	51
GBA	Graham	Barney	Science	14
JKW	Jennie	Kwong	English	42
PTY	Paul	Tyrell	Science	13
SJR	Sarah	Jordan	English	43

a ....

b ....

c ....

4 Name the type of field used to hold unique data that is used to identify each record.

....

5 Name the **three** main data types used in database fields.

1 ....

2 ....

3 ....

6 Explain the most important reasons for using a relational database rather than a flat-file database.

....

....

....

....

7 Sometimes numeric data is not stored in a field with a numeric data type. Explain why this happens and give one example where this would be appropriate.

....

....

....

....

8 Name the sub-types of numeric data described:

a Data is displayed to show today's date. ....

b Data contains only whole numbers. ....

c Data displays a symbol like \$ or £ and often has two decimal places. ....

d Data can contain whole numbers and decimal values. ....

e Data displays the time. ....

9 Name the type of field in a table that will point to the primary key field in another table.

....

10 Explain why *Microsoft Excel* is not suitable for database tasks.

....

....

....

....

11 Explain how you would change the format of a field with a Boolean data type in *Microsoft Excel* from Yes/No to On/Off.

....

....

....

....

....

....

....

....

12 Name and describe the two methods of verification that could be used when new data is typed into a database.

Method 1: ....

Description 1: ....

....

Method 2: ....

Description 2: ....

....

13 Explain the purpose of a database form.

....

....

....

....

....

....

....

....

14 Name the type of questions that, where possible, should be used on a database form.

....

15 Tick three items from the following list that would be suitable for use on a database form with closed questions.

- **a** Text box ☐
- **b** Option group with radio (option) buttons ☐
- **c** List box (drop down list) with limit to list ☐
- **d** Drop down list without limit to list ☐
- **e** Tick box (check box) ☐
- **f** Combo box ☐

16 Explain the purpose of navigation buttons on a database form.

....

....

....

....

....

....

....

....

17 Identify the features of a well-designed data entry form.

....

....

....

....

....

....

....

....

18 Complete the following sentence using the correct terms from the list below:

- query
- chart
- form
- interrogator
- report
- export

Databases like *Microsoft Access* search for data using a .... The easiest method is to use the .... wizard.

19 Identify the character used to allow a wildcard search in a database.

....

20 Identify the criteria that would be used in a Salary field to select all the employees who earn less than or equal to $5,000.00.

....

21 A database contains two fields, *Sales_Price* and *Purchase_Price*. You have been asked to create a new field, calculated at run-time to display the Profit. Identify the formula that you will enter into the *Field*: box within the query.

....

22 The following are extracts from a database.

For each extract, describe the sorting applied to the data:

a		
First name	**Surname**	**Tutor group**
Emily	Wright	11XSJR
Alexander	Terry	11YCAL
Sophie	Clinch	11YVMA
George	Arnold	11YVMA
Rachel	Noles	11XSJR
Thomas	Kleider	11XSJR

b		
First name	**Surname**	**Tutor group**
Alexander	Terry	11YCAL
Emily	Wright	11XSJR
George	Arnold	11YVMA
Rachel	Noles	11XSJR
Sophie	Clinch	11YVMA
Thomas	Kleider	11XSJR

c		
First name	**Surname**	**Tutor group**
Sophie	Clinch	11YVMA
George	Arnold	11YVMA
Alexander	Terry	11YCAL
Emily	Wright	11XSJR
Rachel	Noles	11XSJR
Thomas	Kleider	11XSJR

d		
First name	**Surname**	**Tutor group**
George	Arnold	11YVMA
Sophie	Clinch	11YVMA
Thomas	Kleider	11XSJR
Rachel	Noles	11XSJR
Alexander	Terry	11YCAL
Emily	Wright	11XSJR

a ....

....

....

....

b ....

....

....

....

c ....

....

....

....

d ....

....

....

....

23 Identify, for the subject of IGCSE ICT, the generic meaning of the word 'report'.

....

....

24 Explain where data held in the following sections of a database report is displayed:

a Report Header ....

....

b Page Header ....

....

c Detail ....

....

d Page Footer ....

....

e Report Footer ....

....

25 You are using a mouse to select multiple controls in the Design View of a *Microsoft Access* report. State which key allows you to click on and select more than one control at once.

....

26 State in which section of a database report you would:

a place a calculated control to display the total for a field

....

b place a heading that would appear on every page

....

c add your name at the bottom of the report but not on every page.

....

27 You have designed a report in landscape and it looks like this.

Graham Brown Alloy wheels

Make	Model	Colour	SPrice	Year	Extras	Valet
TVR	Tuscan	Black	£20,305.00	2012	Alloy Wheels Air Conditioning	No
BMW	Z3	Metallic black	£5,635.00	2006	Alloy Wheels	No
Toyota	Celica	Red	£24,695.00	2014	Air Conditioning Alloy Wheels	Yes
Audi	TT	Black	£17,545.00	2013	Central Locking Leather Seats Alloy Whe	No
Ford	Focus	Dark blue	£3,135.00	2009	Alloy Wheels	No

Describe how you could make all of the data in the Extras field fully visible.

28 Describe **two** reasons why reports or queries might be exported into another applications package.

1

2

29 Describe **two** ways that data could be hidden in a report.

1

2 ....

....

....

....

30 Describe why data may be hidden in a report.

....

....

....

....

....

....

....

....

31 Describe how you would change a control on a report to display data as a percentage value.

....

....

....

....

....

....

....

....

32 A calculated control is placed in the report footer of an *Access* report.

a Identify the formula that you would enter in this calculated control to display the average value of the 'Profit' field in an *Access* report.

....

b Name the type of control used to display the text 'Average', next to your calculated control.

....

33 Identify how the data in the following database extracts have been sorted.

a		
First_Name	**Surname**	**Roll_Number**
Arthur	Brown	G_0003
Ali	Dhar	G_0004
Ali	Hussein	G_0005
Stephen	Brown	G_0010
Steven	Cooper	G_0013
Temi	Adediji	G_0008
Li	Xu	G_0009

b		
First_Name	**Surname**	**Roll_Number**
Ali	Dhar	G_0004
Ali	Hussein	G_0005
Ali	Ahmed	G_0014
Li	Xu	G_0009
Stephen	Brown	G_0010
Steven	Cooper	G_0013
Temi	Adediji	G_0008

c		
First_Name	**Surname**	**Roll_Number**
Arthur	Brown	G_0003
Ali	Dhar	G_0004
Ali	Hussein	G_0005
Temi	Adediji	G_0008
Li	Xu	G_0009
Stephen	Brown	G_0010
Steven	Cooper	G_0013

d		
First_Name	**Surname**	**Roll_Number**
Steven	Cooper	G_0013
Stephen	Brown	G_0010
Li	Xu	G_0009
Temi	Adediji	G_0008
Ali	Hussein	G_0005
Ali	Dhar	G_0004
Arthur	Brown	G_0003

e		
First_Name	**Surname**	**Roll_Number**
Li	Xu	G_0009
Ali	Hussein	G_0005
Ali	Dhar	G_0004
Steven	Cooper	G_0013
Stephen	Brown	G_0010
Arthur	Brown	G_0003
Temi	Adediji	G_0008

f		
First_Name	**Surname**	**Roll_Number**
Temi	Adediji	G_0008
Arthur	Brown	G_0003
Stephen	Brown	G_0010
Steven	Cooper	G_0013
Ali	Dhar	G_0004
Ali	Hussein	G_0005
Li	Xu	G_0009

a ....

....

....

....

b ....

....

....

....

c ....

....

....

....

d ....

....

....

....

e ....

....

....

....

f ....

....

....

....

19 Presentations

1 Explain what a presentation is and how it may be used.

....

....

....

....

....

....

....

....

2 State which of the following file types would be most suitable to open as a presentation.

.csv .pdf .txt .zip .gif .rtf .tif

....

3 Explain why a master slide is used when creating a presentation.

....

....

....

....

....

....

....

....

4 **a** Name the top master slide in *Microsoft PowerPoint*.

....

....

b Explain what happens to the objects placed on this slide.

....

....

5 You are to deliver a presentation using a multimedia projector and you need to set the aspect ratio for this presentation.

Explain what is meant by the aspect ratio when working with a presentation.

....

....

....

....

....

....

....

....

6 You have created a presentation and entered your name into the footer area using the top master slide. When you try to show this presentation your name is not visible on any slide.

Describe how you make the footer visible on all slides.

....

....

....

....

....

....

....

....

7 Select the most efficient method of creating a *PowerPoint* presentation by using a source file:

a Set up your master slide/s, then import/open the data from a generic text file

b Import/open the data from a generic text file, then set up your master slide/s

c Set up your master slide/s, then re-type the contents of the text file into the presentation.

....

8 Describe how you would create a chart in *Microsoft Excel* and place this chart on slide 5 of your presentation.

....

....

....

....

....

....

....

....

9 Explain the difference between audience notes and presenter notes for a presentation delivered in a lecture theatre.

....

....

....

....

....

....

....

....

....

....

....

....

....

....

....

....

10 A presentation on e-safety has been created in a corporate house style and contains text, images, transitions and animations. Identify, giving an example for each, two other items that could be included in the presentation to keep an audience interested in it.

....

....

....

....

....

....

....

....

11 Describe the difference between transitions and animations in a presentation.

....

....

....

....

12 A presentation is to be shown as an on-screen carousel in the reception area of a school. Describe how you would set this presentation to loop continuously.

....

....

....

....

....

....

....

....

20 Spreadsheets

1 Explain why you would create a data model.

....

....

....

....

....

....

....

....

2 Complete the following sentences using the correct terms from this list below:

- cell
- cells
- columns
- rows
- sheet
- table
- workbook
- worksheet

A spreadsheet is a two-dimensional .... split into .... and .... It is made up of a number of individual .... Each .... has an address, for example: E9. A spreadsheet is sometimes called a .... or even a .... In *Excel* many sheets can be held within a single ....

3 Identify what the contents of a cell can be.

A cell can hold a ....

A cell can hold a ....

A cell can hold a ....

4 Identify the character that you place in a spreadsheet to start a formula.

....

5 The contents of cells A1 and A2 are multiplied together like this:

	A
1	215412
2	635241
3	1.36839E+11

a Explain why cell A3 shows this answer.

b Describe how you would change this.

6 Explain the difference between absolute and relative cell references.

7 Describe how you would display the formulae used in a spreadsheet rather than the values.

....

....

....

....

8 Identify and name **four** simple mathematical operators used in a spreadsheet.

Operator: .... Name: ....

Operator: .... Name: ....

Operator: .... Name: ....

Operator: .... Name: ....

9 Explain, when using a spreadsheet, the term 'named range'.

....

....

....

....

....

....

....

....

10 Explain, when using a spreadsheet, the term 'function'.

....

....

....

....

11 Cell A4 contains the formula =INT(A6)

Explain the operation of this formula.

....

....

....

....

....

....

12 For the following spreadsheet:

	A	B	C
1	**Rate of pay**	£19.40	
2			
3	**Name**	**Hours worked**	**Pay**
4	David Watson	24	
5	Graham Brown	30	
6	John Reeves	22	
7	Brian Sargent	8	
8	Emily Wright	32	
9	**Total**		
10	**Average**		
11	**Maximum**		
12	**Minimum**		

a Identify the most appropriate *Excel* function to place in cell:

i B9 ....

ii B10 ....

iii B11 ....

iv B12 ....

b Identify the formulae that would be entered in cell:

i C4 ....

ii B9 ....

iii B12 ....

c Explain how you would replicate the formula in cell C4 for each person.

....

....

....

....

13 Describe the operation of each formula and, for each, identify what would be displayed in the cell:

	A
1	64.5519
2	=ROUND(A1,2)
3	=ROUND(A1,0)
4	=ROUND(A1,-1)
5	=INT(A1)

a i Cell A2 – Operation: ....

....

....

ii Result displayed: ....

b i Cell A3 – Operation: ....

....

....

ii Result displayed: ....

c i Cell A4 – Operation: ....

....

....

ii Result displayed: ....

d i Cell A5 – Operation: ....

....

....

ii Result displayed: ....

14 Explain the difference between the COUNT and COUNTA functions.

....

....

....

....

15 Describe the reason for the formula in cell A14 and explain how it works.

	A
1	Number of books read
2	
3	James
4	62
5	Udoka
6	56
7	Lee
8	60
9	Jasmine
10	56
11	Karla
12	23
13	
14	=COUNTA(A3:A12)-COUNT(A3:A12)

....

....

....

....

....

....

....

....

16 A cell contains the function =COUNTIF($F$16:$F$26,"Master craftsman")

Using cell references, explain what this function does.

....

....

....

....

17 A cell contains the function =COUNTIF(JobDescription,"Master craftsman")

Explain what this function does.

....

....

....

....

....

....

18 a A cell contains the function =COUNTIF(JobDescription,$D$3)

Explain what this function does.

....

....

....

....

....

....

b Explain why $D$3 has been used rather than D3.

....

....

....

....

....

....

19 A formula will be placed in cell D2 to count the number of Apples in the list. It will be copied into D3 and D4 to count the Oranges and Pears. What formula should be placed in cell D2?

	A	B	C	D
1			Number of each fruit	
2	Pear		Apple	
3	Pear		Orange	
4	Orange		Pear	
5	Pear			
6	Apple			
7	Orange			
8	Orange			
9	Orange			
10	Pear			
11	Apple			
12	Apple			
13	Apple			
14	Orange			
15	Pear			
16	Apple			
17	Pear			
18	Orange			
19	Apple			
20	Pear			

....

20 What is the most efficient formula to look at the contents of cell A3 and display:

» "Low" if A3 is less than or equal to 2
» "Medium" if A3 is greater than 2 and less than or equal to 7
» "High" if A3 is greater than 7.

....

21 Cell C3 contains the formula =SUMIF($F$3:$F$23,A3,$G$3:$G$23)

Using cell references explain what this formula does.

	A	B	C	D	E	F	G
1	The Manta Conservation Project						
2	Region code	Region	Total income		Date	Region code	Amount
3	AF	Africa	$81.25		13/02/2021	AF	$18.75
4	AS	Asia	$621.88		13/02/2021	AS	$187.50
5	AU	Australasia	$178.13		13/02/2021	NA	$1,247.50
6	EU	Europe	$1,345.00		13/02/2021	EU	$31.25
7	NA	North America	$1,548.13		14/02/2021	NA	$150.63
8	SA	South America	$94.69		14/02/2021	SA	$62.50
9					14/02/2021	AF	$62.50
10					14/02/2021	AS	$31.25
11					14/02/2021	EU	$18.75
12					15/02/2021	AU	$175.00
13					15/02/2021	EU	$1,250.00
14					15/02/2021	NA	$25.00
15					16/02/2021	SA	$32.19
16					16/02/2021	EU	$20.00
17					16/02/2021	NA	$125.00
18					16/02/2021	AS	$68.75
19					17/02/2021	AS	$15.63
20					18/02/2021	AS	$12.50
21					18/02/2021	AU	$3.13
22					19/02/2021	EU	$25.00
23					19/02/2021	AS	$306.25

....

....

....

....

....

....

22 Explain the differences between a HLOOKUP and a VLOOKUP functions.

....

....

....

....

....

....

....

....

23 A cell contains the function =VLOOKUP(D3,$F$2:$G$16,2,0)

Explain what this function does.

....

....

....

....

....

....

....

....

24 The last parameter of a VLOOKUP function can be 0 or 1.

Explain what these values represent.

....

....

....

....

....

....

....

....

25 Describe how you would extract a subset of data within an *Excel* spreadsheet.

....

....

....

....

....

....

....

....

26 Give two methods that may prevent the loss of data integrity when sorting data in a spreadsheet.

Method 1: ....

....

Method 2: ....

....

27 Name four methods of enhancing text in a spreadsheet without changing the font-face or size.

Method 1: ....

Method 2: ....

Method 3: ....

Method 4: ....

28 Explain why you would wrap text in a cell.

29 a Explain the effects of formatting cell A1.

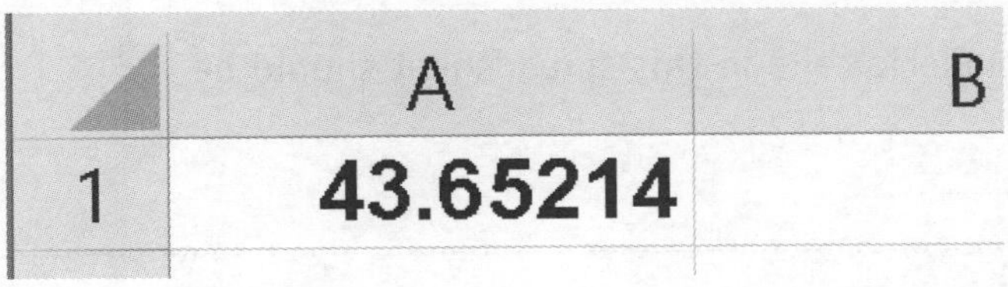

b What would be displayed in cell A1 if it was formatted:

i as an integer

ii to 1 decimal place

iii to 2 decimal places

iv to 3 decimal places

30 Name the **two** types of page orientation:

1

2

31 a Explain how to hide column C.

	A	B	C	D	E	F	G
1	Current jobs			Exchange	Europe	Japan	
2					1.1033	150.974	
3	Customer	Job reference	Estimate	Cost			Increase
4				UK	Europe	Japan	% Increase
5	Avricom	4023	2940	4200	4633.86	634090.8	0.428571429
6	LGY	4122	192000	240000	264792	36233760	0.25
7	Hothouse Design	4123	1050	1500	1654.95	226461	0.428571429
8	Binnaccount	4125	320	475	524.0675	71712.65	0.484375
9	Rootrainer	4126	16240	23200	25596.56	3502596.8	0.428571429

....

....

....

....

b With column C hidden, state how the numeric cells in this spreadsheet should be appropriately formatted.

....

....

....

....

....

....

....

....

32 Explain what conditional formatting does in a spreadsheet.

....

....

....

....

21 Website authoring

1 Explain the term 'website'.

....

....

....

....

2 Identify **three** types of object that can be included in a web page.

1 ....

2 ....

3 ....

3 Name the **three** web development layers.

1 ....

2 ....

3 ....

4 Complete the following text with the name of the web development layer.

a Scripting language is written in the .... layer.

b The structure of a website is created in the .... layer.

c Tables and frames are placed in the .... layer.

d The .... layer can be created in HTML.

e The .... layer can be created in CSS.

f The .... layer can be created in JavaScript.

g A hyperlink is created in the .... layer.

h Images are placed on the web page in the .... layer.

i Font families and sizes are set in the .... layer.

j <head> is placed in the .... layer.

5 Explain the following acronyms:

a HTML ....

....

....

....

....

....

b CSS ....

....

....

....

....

....

6 Identify the file extension used when saving files in:

a HTML ....

b CSS ....

7 State the purpose of the `<html>` tag.

....

....

....

....

8 Name and describe the **two** sections of a web page.

Section 1: ....

Description 1: ....

....

Section 2: ....

Description 2: ....

....

9 Comments are added to markup to help web developers. Write your name as an HTML comment.

....

10 Explain what the following tags represent:

a `<li>` ....

....

....

....

b `<p>` ....

....

....

....

c `<h2>` ....

....

....

....

11 Explain what the following tags represent:

a `<caption>` ....

....

b `<td>` ....

....

c `<tr>` ....

....

d `</tr>` ....

....

e `<table>` ....

....

f `<thead>` ....

....

g `<tfoot>` ....

....

12 Identify the table attribute and values in HTML 5 that make the lines around the edge of a table visible and invisible.

a Lines visible: `<table` .... `>`

b Lines invisible: `<table` .... `>`

c Explain why, even after entering part **a**'s answer, the lines may not appear on the web page.

....

....

13 A table is to be centre aligned and 90 per cent of the width of the browser window. It will show all internal and external lines. Write the table attributes (including embedded CSS) to do this.

`<table` ....`>`

14 Text can be horizontally aligned like this in a web page.

Cell A	Cell B	Cell C	Cell D
This text is just for demonstration purposes and is of no real use in the exercise. It just demonstrates the type of alignment set in each table cell	This text is just for demonstration purposes and is of no real use in the exercise. It just demonstrates the type of alignment set in each table cell	This text is just for demonstration purposes and is of no real use in the exercise. It just demonstrates the type of alignment set in each table cell	This text is just for demonstration purposes and is of no real use in the exercise. It just demonstrates the type of alignment set in each table cell

For each cell, write the CSS to produce these results.

Cell A <td style=" .... ">

Cell B <td style=" .... ">

Cell C <td style=" .... ">

Cell D <td style=" .... ">

15 Cell contents can be aligned vertically like this in a web page:

Cell A	Cell B	Cell C	
This text is just for demonstration purposes and is of no real use in the exercise. It just demonstrates the type of alignment set in each table cell	This text is just for demonstration purposes and is of no real use in the exercise. It just demonstrates the type of alignment set in each table cell	This text is just for demonstration purposes and is of no real use in the exercise. It just demonstrates the type of alignment set in each table cell	This text is just for demonstration purposes and is of no real use in the exercise. It just demonstrates the type of alignment set in each table cell. This text is just for demonstration purposes and is of no real use in the exercise. It just demonstrates the type of alignment set in each table cell

For each cell, write the CSS to produce these results.

Cell A <td style=" .... ">

Cell B <td style=" .... ">

Cell C <td style=" .... ">

16 Explain what each attribute of this HTML tag is used for:

```
<img src="whale1.png" width=300px alt="whale image">
```

....

....

....

....

....

....

....

....

....

....

....

....

17 Some image types are suitable for use in web pages.

In the table below, write Yes or No to state whether each file is an image, a bitmap image, suitable as an image for web authoring and can hold moving images.

File type	Image file	Bitmap image	Image is suitable for web authoring	Suitable for moving images
.bmp				
.gif				
.jpg				
.htm				
.tif				
.css				
.png				

18 In HTML 5 **three** tags are required to place a video.

Identify these tags and the attributes that should be used with each tag.

First tag: ....

....

....

....

Second tag: ....

....

....

....

Third tag: ....

....

....

....

19 State the order of primary colours used in computer output.

....

20 a Identify the largest hexadecimal number that can be stored in a single byte (8 bits).

....

b Write this number again as a decimal value.

....

21 Which symbol tells the browser that a number is in hexadecimal? ....

22 Write the hexadecimal code that will set the background colour of a table to have a green component of 4f (hexadecimal), no red component and full blue component.

```
<table style="background-color: ..................................................................................">
```

23 A trainee creates part of a table like this:

```
<table>
  <tr style="background-color: #0000ff">
    <td><h1 style="color: #0000f0">Hello</h1></td>
  </tr>
```

Evaluate this markup.

....

....

....

....

....

....

....

....

24 Fill in the missing HTML to create this web page:

<h1>Fruit</h1>

< .... >

< .... >Apple < .... >

< .... >Orange < .... >

< .... >Pear < .... >

< .... >Banana < .... >

< .... >Lemon < .... >

< .... >

25 Describe the HTML tags used to create ordered and unordered lists.

....

....

....

....

....

....

....

....

26 Describe a hyperlink.

....

....

....

....

....

....

....

....

27 Describe an HTML anchor.

....

....

....

....

28 a Explain the purpose of the HTML tag <div id="MantaRay">

....

....

....

....

....

....

b Fill in the missing HTML that would be used to move the user from the given text to the correct place in the same web page:

`<h3>If you see a <` .... `>manta ray<` .... `>then please...`

29 Explain what these attributes do when used as part of a hyperlink to open a web page:

a `target="_ self"` ....

....

b `target="_ blank"` ....

....

30 This HTML has been extracted from a web page:

```
<a href="mailto:graham.a.brown@hotmail.co.uk?subject=New%20Workbook">
Click here to contact us</a>
```

Explain what this does.

....

....

....

....

....

....

....

....

31 Explain the purpose, location and use of the <meta> tag.

....

....

....

....

....

....

....

....

32 Apart from 'name', list **two** attributes used within a meta tag.

1 ....

2 ....

33 List **four** values used with the name attribute within a meta tag.

1 ....

2 ....

3 ....

4 ....

34 Give **two** reasons why stylesheets are used with web pages.

1 ....

....

2 ....

....

35 Identify the section of a web page where the stylesheet is attached.

....

36 Explain which stylesheet has the highest priority if more than one stylesheet is attached to a web page.

....

....

37 Identify which HTML attribute allows CSS styles to be embedded in the markup.

....

38 State which symbol is used to separate declarations in CSS. ....

39 Comments are added to a stylesheet to help web developers. Write your name as a CSS comment.

....

40 Identify the following items from this CSS:

```
body  {background-color: #ff0000}
```

a the selector ....

b the declaration property ....

c the declaration value ....

41 Identify the error in each of the following CSS rules:

a `h1  {text-align:centre}`

....

....

b `h2  {font-family:"Arial MT Bold","Arial","sans-serif"}`

....

....

c `h3  {font-weight:italic}`

....

....

d `h4  {font-family:serif,Times,Abril;}`

....

....

e `h5  {color:#ff00fh}`

....

....

f `h6  {font-family:Arial MT Bold,Arial,sans-serif`

....

....

g `p {text-align:justified}`

....

....

h `body {background-image: url("image.jpg") background-repeat:no-repeat}`

....

....

42 Write the CSS needed to place the background image like this.

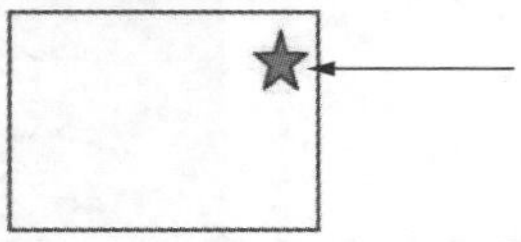

....

43 What character precedes the selector to define a class rather than a style? ....

44 Explain what each line of this CSS does.

```
table       {background-color: #0000ff;
             border-collapse:collapse;
             border-style:solid;
             border-width:4px}
```

Line 1: ....

....

Line 2: ....

....

Line 3: ....

....

Line 4: ....

....

Consolidate understanding of a full range of software functions with further practice questions and activities

This Practical Workbook provides additional support and practice in the practical skills required by the Cambridge IGCSE™ Information and Communications Technology syllabus.

- » **Refine software skills:** includes a series of questions designed to test and develop concepts that underpin practical skills.
- » **Develop understanding and build confidence:** questions will aid preparation for all aspects of examinations.

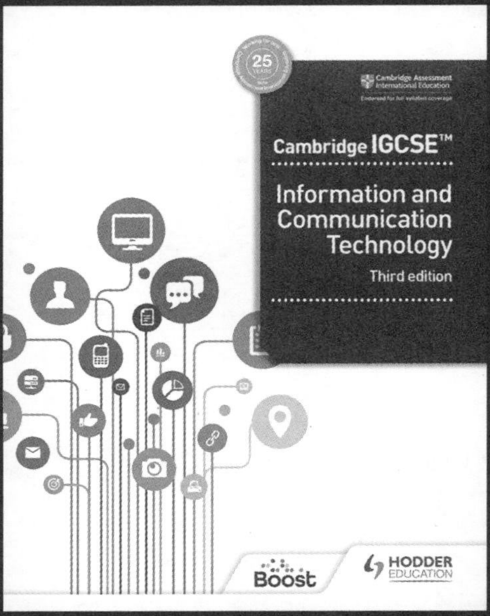

Use with *Cambridge IGCSE™ Information and Communication Technology Student's Book Third Edition*

9781398318540

This resource is endorsed by Cambridge Assessment International Education

- ✓ Provides learner support for the Cambridge IGCSE™ and IGCSE (9-1) Information and Communication Technology syllabuses (0417/0983) for examination from 2023
- ✓ Has passed Cambridge International's rigorous quality-assurance process
- ✓ Developed by subject experts
- ✓ For Cambridge schools worldwide

HODDER EDUCATION
e: education@hachette.co.uk
w: hoddereducation.com

ISBN 978-1-398-31851-9

9 781398 318519

FSC www.fsc.org MIX Paper from responsible sources FSC™ C104740